Easy Green Smoothie Recipe Book for Kids & Adults

Get Your Family Drinking Greens, Fruits & Veggies with Green Reset Formula!

Joanna Slodownik

Published by Green Reset Media

Copyright 2014. All rights reserved.

Disclaimer: This book is not a source of medical information. This publication is designed to provide information about the subject matter covered. The reader is encouraged to seek professional medical advice before taking action. While all attempts have been made to provide effective, accurate information in this book, neither the author nor publisher assume responsibility for errors, inaccuracies, or omissions. The reader assumes the risk and full responsibility for all actions, and the authors will not be held liable for any loss or damage, whether consequential, incidental, special or otherwise, that may result from the information offered in this book.

Table of Contents

Green Reset Formula For Families 5
What's so special about green smoothies? 8
Why Families Should Go Green? 10
Why Not Just Eat More Salad? 13
Starting Your Kids On Green Smoothies 16
The Celery Trick 18
Tips For a Tough Crowd (of Any Age!) 21
Resetting for Your New Green Life: Green Smoothie Basics 23
Green Smoothie Recipes For Beginners 25
More Green Smoothie Combinations 27
The Green Reset: Making it Stick 31
Rich & Creamy Smoothie Recipes 39
Healthy & Decadent Dessert Recipes 43
How to Make a Full Pitcher of Smoothie 46
More tips 51
7 Tips for Successful Smoothie Routine 52
Troubleshooting a Smoothie 54
Top Sweeteners for the Smoothies 57
Boosting Your Smoothies With Sprouts 59
How to Grow Sprouts with Your Kids 61
Is Buying Organic Produce Important? 64
A Note About Blenders 66
Smoothie Ingredients: Cheat Sheet 68
7 Ways to Save Money on Ingredients 70
Q&A 72
More Reading 74
Your Free Gift Is Waiting! 75

Green Reset Formula For Families

If you are looking for the most natural, 100% safe, and absolutely most effective way to help your kids eliminate bad cravings, reprogram their taste buds, and help them truly enjoy healthy foods now and later on as adults, then keep reading.

I'm going to reveal to you a powerful concept that has the potential to transform your life if you apply this knowledge.

I call it the **Green Reset Formula**.

The foods we eat have an enormous impact on our mood, strength, energy level, weight, focus, immunity, and overall well-being. And whole foods—like smoothie ingredients—are some of the healthiest foods you can find.

Most people know that to be healthy and achieve the ideal weight, they should be eating a healthy diet that includes loads of fresh raw fruits and vegetables. However, few people actually do that consistently each and every day. Many people believe that strong willpower, motivation, and clever tricks are needed to make their kids acquire healthy eating habits.

The truth is, you don't need willpower or even strong motivation if you use the proper habits as LEVERAGE.

Proper habits have the power to start a CHAIN REACTION, shifting other patterns as they move through our lives. These habits start a process that, over time, transforms everything.

But aren't habits hard to establish or change? And isn't it hard to resist temptation? Especially since our kids are bombarded more and more with temptations from everywhere.

Besides, how to go about establishing those habits?

The key is to start small, with one simple habit that will create a chain reaction that can significantly influence the success of other habits. It's like making five good decisions for the price of one.

Green Reset Formula helps you jump-start the chain reaction of positive change by incorporating some simple habits into your life. I hope that the information in this book will help you and your family–including your kids–turbo-charge your nutrition, flooding your body with nutrients, helping you improve your health, get more energy and lose weight with these SUPER-EASY, SUPER-FUN, SUPER-FOOD green smoothie recipes!

And it all starts with drinking a green smoothie every day.

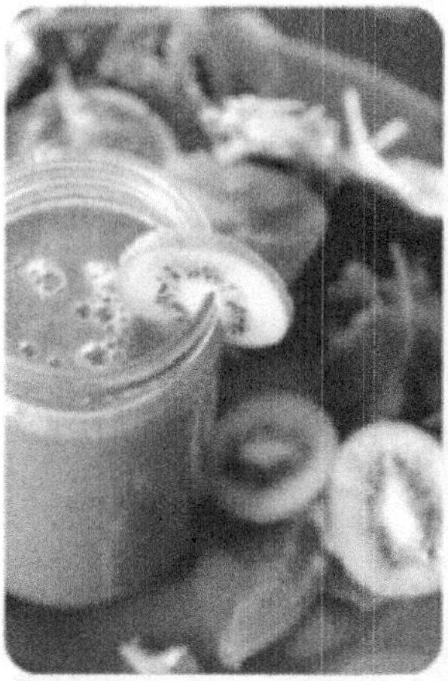
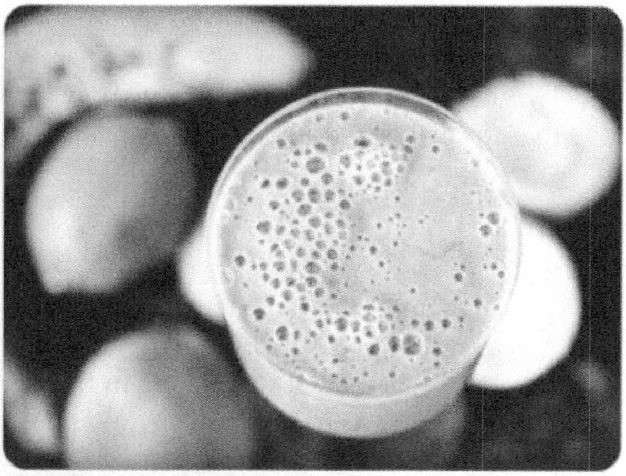
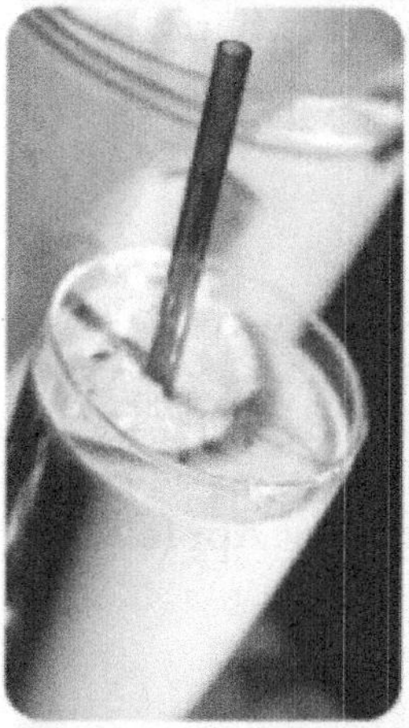
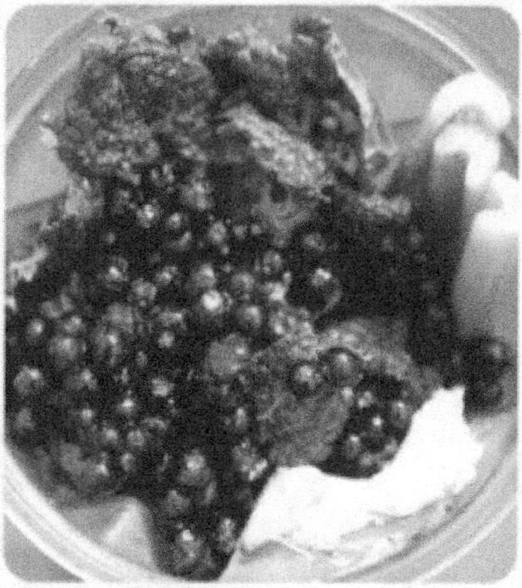
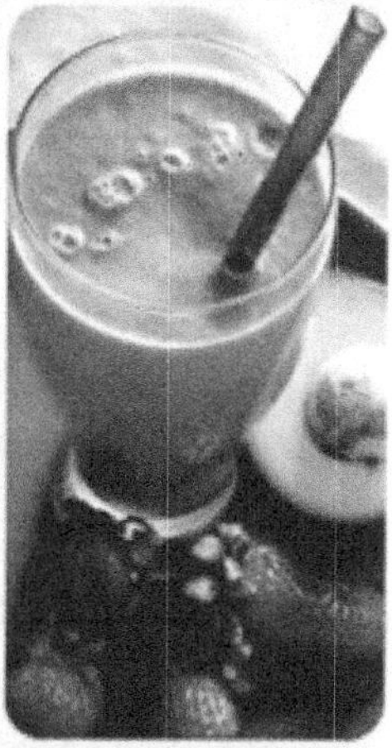
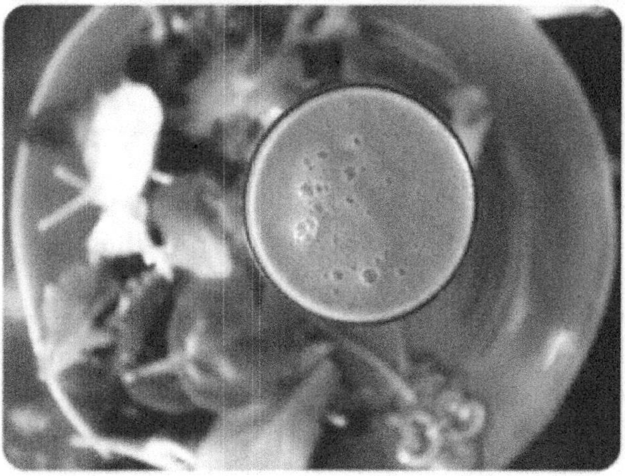
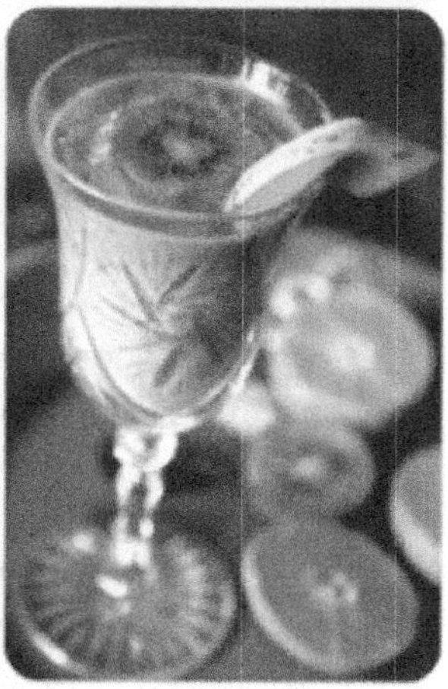

What's so special about green smoothies?

Green smoothies are getting more popular every day, so I don't think there is anyone who doesn't know what they are...

...or is there?

So, just in case, here is a brief overview:

A green smoothie is simply a fruit smoothie with greens and non-starchy veggies added to the mix! In fact, any classic smoothie can be boosted with greens.

Get your kids onto the Green Reset with an easy **Strawberry Banana smoothie**!

> **Green Strawberry Banana Smoothie**
> 1 cup water or fresh orange juice
> 1 cup of mild baby green leaves
> 1 cup strawberries, fresh or frozen
> 2 bananas

Reap the benefits of nutrition with a morning boost of **Apple Kale Lemon** smoothie.

> **Apple, Kale, Lemon Smoothie**
> 2 cups of water, or to desired consistency
> 4 cups of kale
> 4 apples
> ½ lemon juice
> ½ medium avocado for creaminess

Or invite friends over to enjoy a **Pear, Kale, Mint Smoothie** pumped with nutritious flavor!

The truth is most of us (kids or adults) aren't eating a sufficient quantity of natural plant foods. According to the State of the Plate Study on America's Consumption of Fruits & Vegetables, the average person consumes measly 1.8 cups of fruits and vegetables per day or about 660 cups per year[1]. Only 6% of individuals achieve their recommended target for vegetables, while 8% achieve their recommended target for fruit on an average day.

According to Dr. Joel Fuhrman, American children move into adulthood, eating 90% of their caloric intake from dairy products, white flour, sugar, and oil. Then many develop autoimmune illnesses as young adults before heart disease and cancer strikes later. Diseases of nutritional ignorance flourish, but they have not been connected to their cause—childhood diets—until now(2).

Most people consume no or very little greens, and yet on the nutrition front, dark leafy greens, are, calorie for calorie, some of **the most concentrated source of nutrition available**. They deliver a massive amount of vitamins, minerals, phytonutrients, healthy fats, protein, calcium, and, of course, fiber. The darker the leaves, the more nutrients they have.

Green smoothies help ensure that your kids are getting adequate nutrition—fruits, vegetables, greens, with all the fiber, protein, calcium, and other nutrients their growing bodies need. If you have picky eaters, you will especially love how these recipes disguise those all-important "dark" greens.

The beauty of the green smoothie is the ease of preparation and versatility: you can use any fruits and greens you can find! Arugula, bok choy, collards, dandelion, kale, spinach, parsley, romaine lettuce, watercress, sprouted greens, and other edible weeds; plus toss in some herbs: parsley, cilantro, mint, basil, or other. The darker the leaves, the more nutrients they usually have!

Why Families Should Go Green?

Are you struggling to get your children to eat their salads with leafy greens and raw vegetables, or ANY vegetables for that matter?

Would they rather eat candy or processed sugar rather than a piece of fruit?

Are they missing out on all those plant-based vitamins, minerals, antioxidants, healthy carbohydrates, fats, and proteins that every growing body needs for optimum health?

If so, you are certainly not alone. Getting children to eat healthy meals is a concern that most parents have, especially since modern convenience foods marketed to kids are so lacking in nutritional value.

The scary statistics that 40% of the calories children in the United States eat are nutritionally empty! (3)

cola, fries, ice-cream, donuts, pretzels, hot-dogs, soda, muffins, chocolate, candy, chips, sugar, soft-drinks, pies, Twinkies, cookies, cakes

As a result, children are not developing tastes or cravings for the nutritional powerhouse foods they need, including fresh fruits, leafy greens, vegetables, nuts, and seeds.

You want your kids to get a healthy start in life without falling prey to the Standard American Diet (SAD), but if you can't get them to eat their veggies, what can you do?

As a parent, I know how challenging it can be to get kids to eat their veggies — especially the green ones. From me, the answer to this challenge came in a glass of a fruit smoothie packed with fresh leafy greens, a green smoothie.

Most kids love a sweet treat, and making this dessert-like beverage has been a real life-saver.

The Good News Is: Kids Love Green Smoothies!

Kids usually love green smoothies from the first sip and may never realize they are drinking their greens unless you choose to tell them! Plus, making green smoothies is so much fun!

The great thing about green smoothies is that they disguise ingredients that your child might find objectionable. If you can't get your kids to eat spinach or kale in their dinner salad, you will be astonished to see them relishing these very same ingredients in a smoothie.

Making a green smoothie first thing in the morning or as a snack between meals each day will your kids with much-needed nutrition, and it will give you some peace of mind.

Drinking green smoothies is probably the highest-impact activity that you can undertake to improve your health and well-being by spending just 5-10 minutes a day!

Why Not Just Eat More Salad?

But we eat salads every day, why do we need green smoothies?

First of all, if your family is eating large salads every day, congratulations!

However, there are many problems we face when attempting to eat large quantities of raw vegetables (especially greens) every day.

Problem 1: Tiny Portion Sizes

Even if you eat a raw salad, fruits, and raw vegetable snacks every day—chances are your **portion sizes are too small**, probably too small to make a noticeable difference in your or your children's health. Frankly, the serving sizes and nutritional recommendations are pathetically small, and most people don't even meet those recommendations in their diet.

Try putting 1 or 2 lbs. of fresh greens and vegetables on a platter. Tell someone to eat it in a day. It's daunting—virtually impossible unless you're going to spend 30 minutes chopping and 90 minutes chewing. Most people can't spend hours a day preparing their food and trying to get it down, so blending is their best option.

Problem 2: Insufficient Chewing

Most of us don't chew well enough and long enough, so our bodies are unable to absorb as much as they could from the greens and raw vegetables we eat, meaning indigestion and lost nutrients.

When you blend leafy green vegetables, they are a lot easier to digest. The fibers are liquefied, making the nutrients absorb super easy. Blenders "chew" the food for you.

Problem 3: Lack of Time

Preparing a large salad takes a lot of time, from rinsing and spinning the greens, chopping the vegetables, making a dressing, and, most importantly: chewing it all! Who has time every day for such a routine?

Problem 4: Lack of Variety

Plus, green smoothies allow you to **sneak lots of good-for-you ingredients into the diet** that your kids may otherwise avoid. Be honest, when was the last time your child had a kale salad? Collard? Chard or parsley?

The good news is making a smoothie takes only a few minutes; you can even prepare them in advance for 2-3 days and refrigerate or freeze your daily portions, saving time even further.

Plus, drinking your greens in smoothies is a really easy and delicious way to have them, so you will not need to force yourself to consume something that's actually good for you!

How do you like your greens?

Starting Your Kids On Green Smoothies

From my experience, most kids love the smoothies from the get-go. Others, however, may need a little bit of time and convincing.

My son has been drinking green smoothies since he was four, and he loves them (he sometimes asks me why I give them to him *all the time*, LOL).

However, being bold and extra green on your first smoothie attempt may not win new green smoothie lovers. Baby steps are the key to making a smooth transition to developing a taste for greens in your child's smoothie. So make those first few smoothies creamy with a lot of fruit and just a hint of green veggies. Then, with each smoothie you serve, add a little less fruit and a few more green leaves. Also—a little less juice and milk and more filtered water. Your goal is to pack in your child's daily needs for green vegetables.

Here is a technique to get your kids (and yourself) to eat a lot of greens. You can use this method for many different things; for example, it's very effective with exercising.

It's called the "**Foot in the Door Technique.**"

If your child refuses to drink green smoothies, start by making smoothies that don't look green at all. Such as the **Mixed Berry Blast,** which hides the green with bright berry colors.

> **Mixed Berry Blast Smoothie**
> 2 cups water or non-dairy milk
> 1 cup mixed berries, frozen
> 2-4 cups greens
> 1 apple, cored and chopped
> 2-3 stalks of celery
> 1 banana
> 1/4 small avocado
> 1 cup cooked grains

Start with preparing mostly sweet smoothies with lots of fruits or natural sweeteners. Children naturally love the sweet taste of ripe fruit. A great one to start with is the **Kale Berry Banana**.

Kale, Berry, Banana Smoothie
2 cups of water
2 bananas
1 cup of strawberries or blueberries or raspberries
2 celery stalks
4 leaves kale

Or, for something thicker and more filling, try the **Cinnamon Banana Blast Smoothie!**

Cinnamon Banana Blast Smoothie
1 1/2 cup water
2-4 cups baby spinach or kale
1/2 cup any type cooked whole grain
1 ripe banana 1/2 teaspoon cinnamon
1 tablespoon walnuts

The Celery Trick

For truly suspicious eaters, start by introducing celery in green smoothies. Celery hardly changes the color or taste of the smoothie and would be a great way to get children to start eating more of this nutrient-rich vegetable. Here are some first recipes for celery:

Strawberry Banana with Celery Smoothie
1cup water or fresh orange juice
1 celery stalk
1 cup strawberries, fresh or frozen
2 bananas

Banana-Berry with Celery Smoothie
1-2 cups of water or coconut water
1 celery stalk
3/4 cup of frozen mixed berries (or fresh raspberries or blueberries)
1 banana (ripe and peeled)
¼ avocado

Strawberry Pineapple with Celery Smoothie
1 cup water
1 celery stalk
1 cup fresh pineapple cubes
1/2 cup strawberries
1 banana
One to two drops of vanilla essence

Blueberry Pudding
1 cup of water
1 stalk of celery
2 cups blueberries, frozen
1 banana

This is a thick smoothie that you can eat with a spoon, or add more water to desired consistency.

You may start with a half or even a quarter stalk of celery.

Another helpful tip is to offer the smoothie when your child is slightly hungry and thirsty, for example, right after physical activity.

The critical part is getting your foot in the door. Your child may be suspicious about what is exactly in the smoothie, but it's your choice to tell her what is inside the blender.

Even if they don't love it right away, they will probably not hate it either.

Once your child gets used to the celery, start adding small—and hard to detect—quantities of other greens.

Young, tender greens are better, that's why I recommend baby spinach in my recipes. Iceberg lettuce, although not very green at all, can be used too.

If the color is a concern, adding color-changing ingredients, such as blueberries, will also help mask the green that some children may find problematic.

With time, everyone in your home should get used to the taste, and even prefer it over the no-veggie version, which may start to seem too sweet and lack certain tartness. Our taste buds are really quite adaptable!

So, remember, a great green to use for starter green smoothies is celery because it doesn't make the smoothie look overly green. And it's a mild flavor when mixed with fruit.

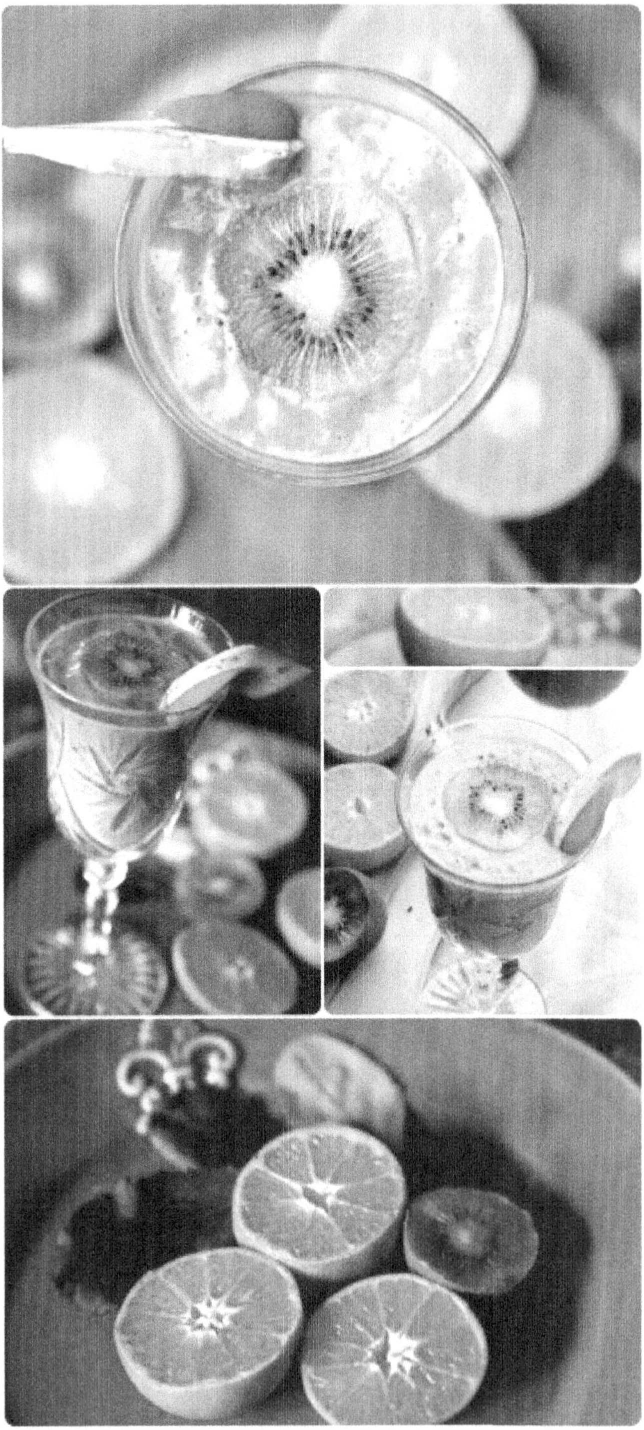

Tips For a Tough Crowd (of Any Age!)

Make the whole routine fun. For young children, conceive a cool name for your smoothies. Princess's Nectar, Magic Potion, Ninjago Blaster, Green Power Ninja Smoothie, Beyblade Master's Smoothie, Shrek's Favorite Smoothie, Persimmon Paradise, Enter the Dragon, Transformer's Fuel—let your imagination go wild! Ask your kids for ideas.

Be a role model. I cannot stress the importance of being a role model for your kids enough. Food preferences and tastes form early in life, and children learn to eat the diets eaten by their parents. Don't expect your children to pick up healthy habits if you don't follow them yourself. If you are eating unhealthy foods, be honest with yourself about the kinds of food messages you're sending. That's why I encourage you to embark on the Green Reset routine as a whole family.

Let them help you prepare the smoothies. What kid doesn't love gadgets? Let them use your blender to make smoothies and other recipes with fruits and vegetables. Use proper supervision, of course.

Take your kids food shopping. Let them pick out the fruits and vegetables. Let them smell the produce and admire the colors.

Use a pretty glass with a straw and a cocktail drink umbrella. If you have a colored glass—it may work even better, because it will mask the real color of the drink.

Require green smoothies before the child eats other things, and be consistent.

My son drinks a green smoothie first thing in the morning before he eats anything else. He usually gets another glass as a snack during the day.

Educate your children (and yourself) about the benefits of eating a diet rich in whole plant foods. Explain it to them in simple terms. You may be surprised by how eager they are to learn. I recommend Dr.

Joel Fuhrman's work, starting with his book "Disease-Proof Your Child" and "Eat to Live."

Make smoothie into a popsicle. Pour into a popsicle container and freeze.

Praise your child for drinking green smoothies. Scientific research proves that praising children for proper food choices, enforces these choices. It really works!

If nothing is working, consider a reward system. I am not a big fan of reward systems, but hey, do whatever works! If your child is highly defiant, and all other methods have failed, you may find that using some kind of incentive is effective. Just, please don't use junk food as treats for reinforcing good eating habits!

Resetting for Your New Green Life: Green Smoothie Basics

When your kids are just starting with the green smoothies, you may want to add just a little bit of mild-tasting greens (such as celery, young spinach, or lettuce), to let their taste buds get used to the taste. (See my section on the Celery Trick.)

Start adding more greens of various kinds gradually, in small quantities.

Greens to add to your smoothies: spinach, arugula, Swiss chard, dandelion, kale, collard greens, various lettuces, as well as herbs—whatever you can find in the store or your garden.

Young, tender greens are better. Iceberg lettuce, although not very green at all, can be used too.

There are unlimited variations, but I recommend not adding too many ingredients per smoothie. Simple is usually better.

By experimenting with different combinations, you will be able to come up with recipes that you and your whole family will love.

Add sweet, ripe fruit (fresh or frozen). Some of the most delicious fruits for green smoothies are bananas, pears, peaches, nectarines, mangoes, strawberries, pineapple, blueberries, raspberries, and apples.

To add more calories and nutrients, add raw nuts, raw seeds, nut butter, seed butter, non-dairy milk, oats or other cooked grains, raw seeds, and dried fruit (for sweetness).

Some fruit and green combinations you may want to try first:

> **Green Strawberry Banana Smoothie**
> **Green Strawberry Pineapple Smoothie**
> **Blueberry Pudding**
> **Kiwi-Mint-Spinach Smoothie**

Green Piña Colada Smoothie
Pineapple-Strawberry Smoothie
Parsley-Pear-Avocado Smoothie

Add 1-2 cups of water or other liquid (freshly squeezed juice, almond milk, coconut water, etc.) and blend until very smooth. Adjust proportions to your child's liking.

Fruits are added for sweetness, so make sure they are really RIPE, especially bananas. Ripe bananas should have brown spots on their skin.

Blend, pour into a glass, and enjoy!

Green Smoothie Recipes For Beginners

Each smoothie recipe makes about a quart or two servings, sometimes more or less, depending on your produce and how accurately you commit to measuring. Measuring produce, especially greens, can be tricky and will yield different results depending on how tightly packed they are, whether they're chopped, fresh or frozen, etc. Adjust the amount of greens depending on your audience, starting with a little, and boosting it with more as their taste-buds adjust. Add more or less liquid depending on your preference for thicker or thinner smoothies, and a few pieces of ice, if you want it chilled.

Green Strawberry Banana Smoothie
1 cup water or fresh orange juice
1 cup of mild baby green leaves (spinach, lettuce, kale, chard, bok choy, or collard)
1 cup strawberries (or other berries), fresh or frozen
2 bananas

Green Strawberry Pineapple Smoothie
1 cup of water
1 cup of mild baby green leaves (spinach, lettuce, kale, chard, bok choy, or collard)
1 cup fresh pineapple cubes
1/2 cup strawberries
1 banana
One to two drops of vanilla essence

Kiwi-Mint Green Smoothie
1 cup of water, almond milk, or other non-dairy milk
1/2 cup mild greens (spinach, lettuce, kale, chard, bok choy, or collard)
2 kiwis, peeled
1/4 small lime, peeled
1 banana, peeled
5 to 10 mint leaves (optional, to taste)

Green Piña Colada Smoothie
13.5-oz can of coconut milk
1/2 bunch of spinach, kale or collard greens, stems removed (4-5 large leaves)
4 cups of fresh pineapple cut into pieces or frozen pineapple chunks
1 banana
a few pieces of ice, if you want it chilled

Pineapple-Blueberry Smoothie with Ginger

1 cup of water (more or less, to desired consistency)
1 cup leaves of spinach or other leafy greens
1 cucumber, peeled
1 cup freshly cut pineapple, or frozen pineapple chunks
1 cup blueberries, fresh or frozen
1 ripe banana (optional)
a piece of fresh ginger (optional, it gives the smoothie nice "zing" that I love)

Apple Celery Smoothie
1 cup of water
2 celery stalks
½ medium avocado
1 apple, peeled and cored
1 banana

Parsley Pear Green Smoothie
1 cup of water
1/2 small bunch parsley
½ medium avocado
2 pears

Blend well and enjoy!

More Green Smoothie Combinations

As you get more familiar with taste of green smoothies, start increasing the amount of smoothie that you and your child drink, with more greens added to the mix. Each of these smoothie recipes makes about a quart and a half to two quarts, more or less, depending on your produce and how accurately you commit to measuring. Adjust the amount of greens depending on your audience, starting with a little, and boosting it with more as their taste-buds adjust. Add more or less liquid depending on your preference for thicker or thinner smoothies, and a few pieces of ice, if you want it chilled.

Spinach, Apple, Banana Smoothie
1 1/2 cup of water, or to desired consistency
4 cups loosely packed greens (spinach, lettuce, kale, chard, bok choy, or collard)
2 stalks celery
1 apple, cored
2 bananas

Green Apple, Banana, Lime Smoothie
1 1/2 cup of water, or to desired consistency
4 cups loosely packed greens (spinach, lettuce, kale, chard, bok choy, or collard)
2 apples
1/2 whole lime with peel
2 bananas

Green Raspberry, Banana, Celery Smoothie
1 1/2 cup of water, or enough water to blend into desired consistency
4 cups loosely packed greens (spinach, lettuce, kale, chard, bok choy, or collard)
2 celery stalks
1/2 cup of raspberries
1/2 cup of strawberries
2 bananas

Romaine Lettuce, Pineapple, Mango Smoothie
2 cups of water, or to desired consistency
1 small pineapple, peeled, cored, and chopped
1 large mango, peeled, cored, and chopped
1 small head romaine lettuce
a tiny piece of fresh ginger

Kale, Berry, Banana Smoothie
2 cups of water, or to desired consistency
4 leaves kale
2 celery stalks
2 bananas
1 cup of strawberries or blueberries or raspberries

Lettuce, Apple, and Mango Smoothie
2 cups of water, or to desired consistency
2-4 cups leaves of green leaf lettuce
2 ripe mangoes, peeled and pit removed
2 apples
1 banana

Arugula, Lettuce, Pear Smoothie
2 cups of water, or to desired consistency
1 small bunch of arugula leaves
1 banana
2 pears
1/2 cup frozen raspberries

Spinach, Celery, Mango Smoothie
1 cup water, or to desired consistency
2 cups of spinach
2 stalks celery
2 sweet yellow mangos

Dandelion Smoothie
1 cup water, or to desired consistency
1/2 bunch dandelion
1/2 small watermelon
1/2 cup strawberries
1 cup of grapes

Kale, Strawberry, Peach Smoothie
2 cups of water, or to desired consistency
1 small bunch green kale
1 pint strawberries
3 small peaches

Peach, Spinach Smoothie
2 cups of water, or to desired consistency
4 cups spinach leaves
2 celery stalks
6 peaches

Apple, Kale, Lemon Smoothie
2 cups of water, or to desired consistency
4 cups of kale
4 apples
½ lemon juice
½ medium avocado for creaminess

Pear, Kale, Mint Smoothie
2 cups of water, or to desired consistency
4 cups of kale
½ bunch of mint
4 ripe pears

Romaine, Strawberry, Banana Smoothie
2 cups water, or to desired consistency
½ bunch Romaine
2 cups strawberries
2 bananas

Romaine Lettuce, Honeydew Smoothie
2 cups water, or to desired consistency
6 to 8 leaves of Romaine lettuce
1/2 medium honeydew

Papaya, Orange, Lettuce Smoothie
2 cups water, or to desired consistency
1/2 head romaine lettuce
2 stalks of celery

1 cup papaya
1 orange
1 cup of red grapes

Grapes, Lettuce, Celery Smoothie
1 cup of water
1/2 head romaine lettuce
2 stalks of celery
1 orange
1 bunch red grapes

The Green Reset: Making it Stick

Fast and Filling Meals

These rich and creamy smoothies are a complete meal, not just your ordinary green smoothie. This is because they contain more filling carbs, proteins, and fats, so you get your breakfast or lunch all in one glass and don't have to make additional meals or snacks. If you are having trouble in the morning preparing multiple breakfasts, lunches, or snacks, this drink will give you and your kids everything they need.

These smoothies are not intended to be a low-calorie drink as they are a complete meal. It's important to get a substantial amount of calories at the start of the day as that's when we need the most energy and keeping off hunger pangs and cravings for unhealthy foods is essential.

You can tweak the ingredients to suit your child's taste, your budget, and food availability. Play around with these recipes and see what works for your family!

How to Make Green Smoothies More Filling

There are seven basic ingredients:

Liquids (water, non-dairy milk or juice)

Greens (Spinach, Chard, Collard Greens, Lettuce, Kale or other mild greens. Also, green veggies, such as celery stalks, cucumbers, etc.)

Fruit (Add any fruit you like, you don't have to worry about adding creamy fruit as the oats provide the creaminess)

Carbs (Oats, Quinoa, Buckwheat, Cooked sweet potato or winter squash)

Seeds or nuts (Any raw seeds or nuts can be added, e.g., chia, flax, hemp, sunflower, pumpkin seeds, walnuts, pecans, etc.)

Sweetener (Dried fruits, agave nectar, stevia, etc. Optional.)

Herbs, spices & superfoods (Fresh ginger, lemon peel, cinnamon, vanilla, parsley, cilantro, spirulina, maca, etc.)

Basically, any recipe can be adjusted to be more filling and keep you satisfied longer, by adding one of the following ingredients:

* **Substitute part of water with non-dairy milk:** oat, rice, soy, almond, hemp, coconut water, or raw nut or seed milk. Sample recipe featuring non-dairy milk:

Banana Almond Dessert
2 very ripe bananas, frozen
2 tablespoons almond butter
1/2 celery stalk
2 chopped, pitted dates
1 cup water or almond milk

* **Add avocado.** In addition to healthy fats, it adds a wonderful creaminess to smoothies. Sample recipe with avocado:

Minty Cream of Spinach Smoothie
2 cups of non-dairy milk (oat, rice, soy, almond, hemp, coconut, or other)
1 cup spinach, tightly packed or 2 cups loosely packed
1 cup oats or quinoa
1 apple, cored
1 avocado, pitted
1 lime, juiced
10 mint leaves

Banana Almond Butter Smoothie

Vegetarian, vegan, dairy free, egg free, refined sugar free, wheat free, soy free (if not using soy milk), nut free (if using seed butter)

ADD NUT OR SEED BUTTER (ALMOND, PEANUT, HAZELNUT, MACADAMIA, CASHEW, SUNFLOWER, PUMPKIN, SESAME, ETC.) TO YOUR SMOOTHIE FOR **DELICIOUSLY RICH, CREAMY AND DISTINCTLY BUTTERY DRINK.**

The Good:
- protein
- healthful fats
- fiber
- vitamins & minerals
- phytochemicals

Safety First. If your allergies force you to keep your distance from all nuts, seed (pumpkin, sunflower) and soy nut butters are excellent alternatives.

* **Add 1/4 cup nuts or seeds, such as walnuts, almonds, brazil nuts, hazelnuts, pumpkin seeds, sunflower seeds, hemp seeds, or flax seeds.** Pre-soaking your seeds and nuts is recommended, but not required. Be aware that nuts and seeds require longer blending, or your smoothie may have a somewhat chunky texture. If your blender cannot

handle the job, you may use a coffee grinder to grind the nuts and seeds before adding them to the smoothie or use nut or seed butter instead.

Ingredients such as chia, flax, and hemp are often called superfoods. It means that they are perfect foods and have all essential amino acids. They have the omega fatty acids that we need, both 3, 6, and in some cases, 9. They have fiber, antioxidants that ward off free radicals, and they also serve as thickening agents. They give the smoothies that nice, silky-rich texture, instead of just having blended bits and pieces of greens with juice. Adding chia seeds or hemp or flax helps the smoothie to expand, giving it that silkiness. It also helps you to feel full. Sample recipes:

Strawberry Oat Smoothie with Pumpkin Seeds
1 cup oat milk
1 cup water
1 cup instant oats
2 tablespoons pumpkin seeds
1 cup strawberries
2 cups spinach
2 large stalks of celery
1 banana

Sesame Mango Smoothie
1 cup non-dairy milk
1 cup water
1 cup instant oats or cooked quinoa
1/4 cup pitted dates (pre-soaked for a smoother blend)
2 tablespoons sesame seeds (or use tahini paste)
2 cups romaine lettuce
1 cup mango chunks
1 banana

* Add 1/4 cup up to 1 cup of whole grains: oats, cooked brown rice, quinoa or other whole grains.

Oats don't need to be cooked (I use the one-minute quick oats). Other grains will need to be prepared in advance. If you have leftover grains, even better! Sample recipe with whole grains:

Lime-Oats Smoothie
2 cups non-dairy milk
2 bananas, fresh or frozen
2 cups leafy greens (spinach, Swiss chard, kale, etc.)
1 handful of parsley
2 tablespoons sunflower seeds
¼ cup of dates (or any other dried fruit)
1 cup oats
juice and zest of 4 limes

* Add 1/2 cooked sweet potato.

Sample recipe featuring sweet potato:

Peachy Sweet Potato Smoothie
3 oranges (or 2 cups of orange juice)
1 cup leafy greens (baby spinach, lettuce, chard, kale, collards or bok choy)
4 peaches (or 2 mangoes)
1 apple, cored and peeled
½ juice lime
1 cup sweet potato, peeled and cubed (cooked and cooled)

* Add ½ to 1 cup of tofu. Sample recipe with tofu:

Raspberry Mousse
1 packet silken tofu, drained (14 ounces)
1 orange, peeled
1 ½ cup frozen raspberries
1/4 avocado dash of vanilla extract or vanilla paste
dash of sea salt
2 tablespoons agave, or more to taste

* Add 2-3 tablespoons of seed or nut butter. Almond, peanut, cashew butter, tahini, etc. Avocado, whole nuts, and nut butters and milks will add some healthy fats to your smoothies– adding any of this will make your smoothie deliciously rich, creamy, and distinctly buttery.

These fats improve the absorption of nutrients, as well as will slow down the release of the fruit sugar into your bloodstream. Don't overdo it, use these ingredients sparingly. Sample recipe:

Banana Almond Butter Smoothie
1 1/2 cup almond milk
2-3 cups mild greens
3 bananas
2 tablespoons almond butter
1 cup peaches or other fruit, fresh or frozen
1/2 teaspoon vanilla butter or extract

Notes:

When buying nut butter or seed butter, check the label. Be sure to check the label before selecting a nut or seed butter. While all nut butters contain around 100 calories per tablespoon, not all nut butters contain healthful ingredients. Many brands contain only ground-up nuts, but some contain added salt and sugar. Some use partially hydrogenated oil—a source of unhealthy trans fats.

Watch the calories. While nuts are considered "nutritional powerhouses," they're also high in calories. Children require more calories from fats than adults, so if you make a pitcher for the whole family and are concerned about the calories, pour your smoothies first, and then add more butter for your children and blend again. Don't let the fear of fat keep you away from trying nut butters, however. Eating just two ounces of nuts weekly can lower your risk of heart disease.

Safety first. If allergies are a concern, seed nut butters are excellent alternatives. Sunflower seed butter is high in heart-healthy polyunsaturated fats. Soy nut butter (which tastes similar to peanut butter) is higher in protein and lower in fat than the average nut butter. If your child's nut allergies are severe, ask your doctor to test for potential soy or seed intolerance before trying these options. If you have a family history of nut allergies, play it safe. It's essential to check with your doctor if you or your child has even a minor allergic reaction to nuts.

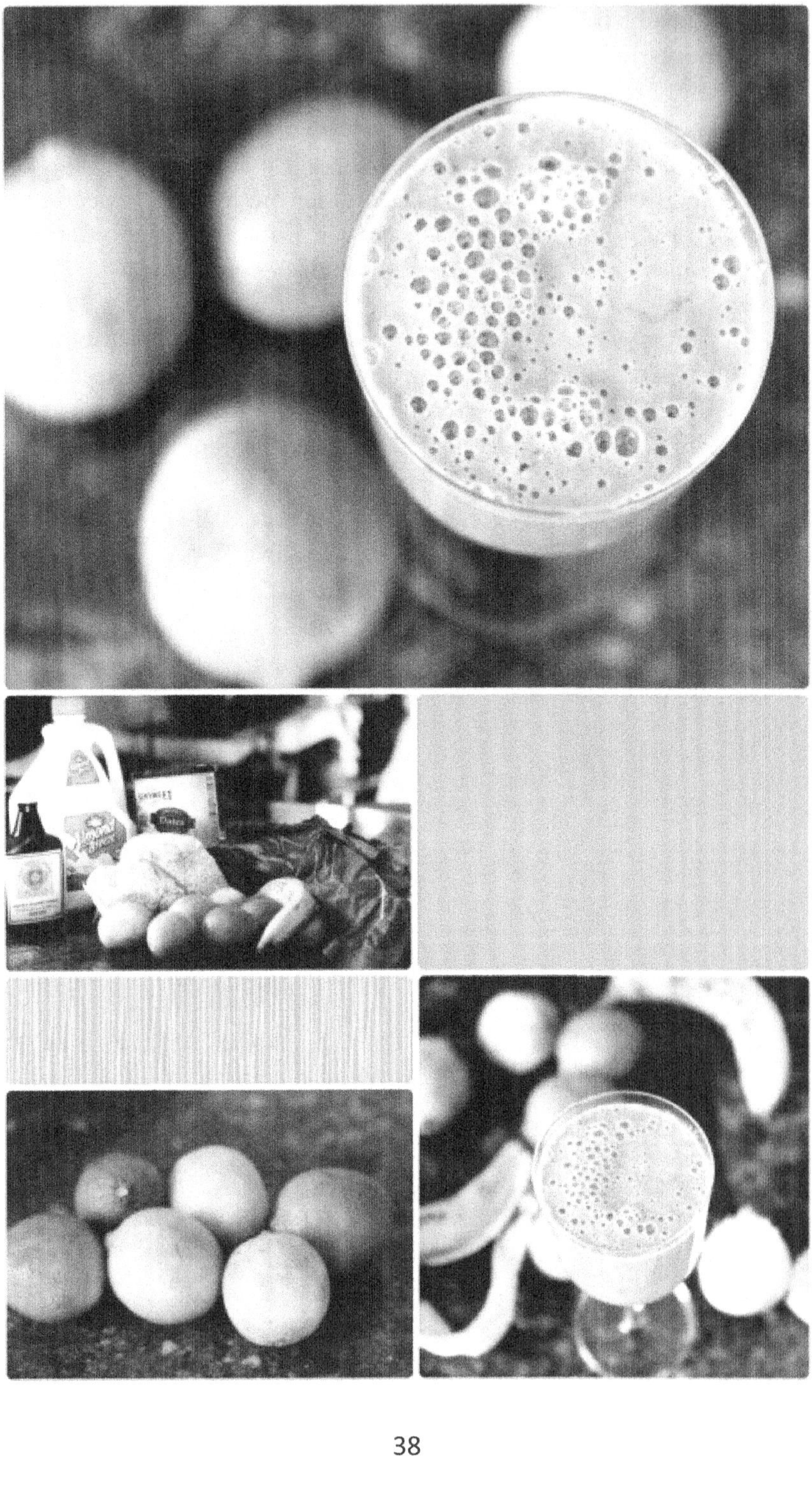

Rich & Creamy Smoothie Recipes

Banana Almond Butter Smoothie
1 1/2 cup almond milk, or any other dairy-free milk
2-3 cups mild greens, such as spinach or mixed greens
3 bananas
1 cup peaches or other fruit, fresh or frozen
2 tablespoons almond butter (or nut butter of your choice)
1/2 teaspoon vanilla butter or extract
Yields about 1.5 quart

Cinnamon Banana Blast Smoothie
1 1/2 cup water (or more for a thinner smoothie)
2-4 cups baby spinach or kale
1/2 cup any type cooked whole grain
1 ripe banana
1/2teaspoon cinnamon
1 tablespoon walnuts
Yields about 1 quart

Mixed Berry Blast Smoothie
2 cups water or non-dairy milk (or more for a thinner smoothie)
2-4 cups greens (kale, collards, parsley, or other)
2-3 stalks of celery
1/4 small avocado
1 cup mixed berries, frozen
1 apple, cored and chopped
1 banana
1 cup cooked grains
Yields about 2 quarts

Avocado Vanilla Smoothie
1 cup almond milk
1/2 avocado
2 chopped, pitted dates
2 teaspoons vanilla extract
2 teaspoons agave nectar

Combine all ingredients and blend until very smooth.
Yields about a half quart

Spicy Plum Oat Smoothie
2 cups non-dairy milk(or more for a thinner smoothie)
1-2 cups spinach
8 plums
1 banana
1 cup oats, cooked quinoa, or brown rice
½ cup dates
½ teaspoon vanilla
1 teaspoon fresh ginger
Yields about 1.5 quarts

Peachy Green Smoothie
1 cup non-dairy milk (or more for a thinner smoothie)
1 cup spinach
3 small peaches, pitted
1 tablespoon sesame seeds
1/4 cup dried apricots (pre-soaked for a smoother blend)
1/2 cup instant oats
sprinkle with a dash of cinnamon before serving
Yields about 1 quart

Strawberry Oat Smoothie
1 cup oat milk or other non-dairy milk
1 cup water, or to desired consistency
1 cup strawberries
2 cups spinach
2 large stalks of celery
1 banana
1 cup instant oats
2 tablespoons pumpkin seeds
Yields about 2 quarts

Minty Cream of Spinach Smoothie
2 cups non-dairy milk (oat, rice, soy, almond, hemp, coconut water or other)
1 cup spinach, tightly packed or 2 cups loosely packed (or other

mild greens)
1 cup oats or quinoa
1 apple, cored
1 avocado, pitted
1 lime, juiced
10 mint leaves
Yields about 1.5 quart

Sesame Mango Smoothie
1 cup non-dairy milk
1 cup water, or to desired consistency
2 cups romaine lettuce
1 cup mango chunks
1 banana
1 cup instant oats or cooked quinoa
1/4 cup pitted dates (pre-soaked for a smoother blend)
2 tablespoons sesame seeds (or use tahini paste)
Yields about 1.5 quart

Broccoli Blitz Smoothie
2 cups water or non-dairy milk, or more to desired consistency
2 cups spinach
1 cup of broccoli (florets and/or stems), or broccoli rabe
2 oranges, peeled and quartered
2 cups pineapple, chopped
1 banana, frozen
2 cups frozen mixed berries
1 cup oats or quinoa
maple syrup or agave to taste (optional)
Yields about 2.5 quarts

Lime-Oats Smoothie
2 cups non-dairy milk
2 bananas, fresh or frozen
2 cups leafy greens (spinach, Swiss chard, kale, etc.)
1 handful of parsley
2 tablespoons sunflower seeds (or other seeds or nuts that you have)
¼ cup of dates (or any other dried fruit)

1 cup oats, quinoa, or brown rice
juice and zest of 4 limes
Yields about 1.5 quart

Peachy Sweet Potato Smoothie
3 oranges (or 2 cups of orange juice)
1 cup leafy greens (baby spinach, lettuce, chard, kale, collards or bok choy)
4 peaches (or 2 mangos)
1 apple, cored and peeled
1/2 juice lime
1 cup sweet potato, peeled and cubed (cooked and cooled)
Yields about 1.5 quart

Blend all ingredients until very smooth, pour, and enjoy!

These smoothies are a complete meal, with plenty of fiber, protein, complex carbohydrates, calcium, antioxidants, fruits, veggies, greens, and delicious flavor!

Healthy & Decadent Dessert Recipes

When making blended desserts, I usually don't include greens in them, so technically, they don't belong in this book. However, I wanted to include a few recipes, at least to get you started with some simple combinations. My three favorite base ingredients are frozen bananas, avocado, tofu, and chia seeds.

Although adding greens or vegetables to a dessert may seem wicked, if you don't overdo it, your child will not even notice.

I would stick to avocado or celery, to avoid changing the color.

Preparing the dessert with frozen fruit or adding some ice will make the taste of greens even less noticeable.

Banana Almond Dessert
2 very ripe bananas, frozen
2 tablespoons almond butter
1/2 celery stalk
2 chopped, pitted dates
1 cup water or almond milk
Combine all ingredients and blend until very smooth.

Frozen Mango Banana Smoothie
3 medium frozen bananas or more, depending on desired thickness
1 mango
1/4 medium avocado
2 teaspoons maple syrup or agave nectar
1 cup water or almond milk

Add frozen bananas and blend until smooth. Enjoy immediately!

Easiest Ever Chocolate Mousse
1 large avocado (3/4—1 cup mashed)
1/4—1/3 cup vegan hot cocoa mix (sweetened)
a pinch of salt
a few drops of vanilla extract

Mash up the avocado with hot cocoa mix. Process in a food processor until smooth with a pinch of salt and a few drops of vanilla.
Serve in pretty glass containers decorated with slices of banana, chocolate chips, coconut flakes, or whatever else you have in your pantry!

Strawberry Mousse
1 packet silken tofu, drained (14 ounces)
1 orange, peeled
2 cups strawberries, frozen
2 tablespoons maple syrup or agave nectar (or to taste)
1 teaspoon fresh lemon juice (orange juice can be used too)
a dash of vanilla extract
a dash of salt (optional)
Makes 4 servings.

Raspberry Mousse
1 packet silken tofu, drained (14 ounces)
1 orange, peeled
1.5 cup frozen raspberries
1/4 avocado
dash of vanilla extract or vanilla paste
dash of sea salt
2 tablespoons agave, or more to taste (or another sweetener)

Place all the ingredients in a blender or food processor and puree until creamy. Pour the mousse into parfait glasses or individual dessert bowls and chill.

Optionally, you may use carob powder for part of the chocolate. If using unsweetened cocoa powder, add a few tablespoons of brown sugar. Makes 4 servings.

Vanilla Chia Seed Pudding
1/2 cup chia seeds
2 cups non-dairy milk
1 celery stalk
cup peaches or mango, frozen
1 teaspoon vanilla bean paste or vanilla extract
2 tablespoons pure maple syrup or agave nectar (or 3 dates)

Combine all of the ingredients in the blender and blend until a uniform texture is achieved. Keep refrigerated or chill overnight.

Here are some optional ingredients for garnish to make your dessert into a truly elegant affair:

- dark chocolate chips or chocolate shavings
- shredded coconut
- pecans, walnuts, or other nuts, chopped or whole
- freshly grated orange zest
- cinnamon or nutmeg
- sliced banana
- sliced strawberries
- whole blueberries or other berries
- crushed vegan cookies or Grahams
- brown sugar
- a drizzle of agave or maple syrup
- cashew cream, soy or coconut whip on top

How to Make a Full Pitcher of Smoothie

You're probably thinking, *"I don't need to make a full pitcher!"* You don't think your child could drink that much smoothie all at once? Well, of course, not.

However, the idea is that your entire family will be adopting this new habit, so the whole pitcher is for you, your spouse, and your kids.

Plus, you don't have to drink it all in one sitting. You can store it in the fridge for later or pour it into a plastic bottle and take it with you, or freeze it. It will cut your preparation even further.

To make a full pitcher of smoothie follow this simple template recipe:

1/3 liquid+ 1/3 greens + 1/3 fruits = a pitcher of smoothie

(Perhaps you will even need to make two or three, depending on the size and appetites of your family members.)

I usually add all the ingredients at once to make my smoothie in the Vitamix. However, if you have a less powerful blender, and especially if you're adding dry ingredients, such as nuts, oats or seeds, you may start gradually in three steps as follows:

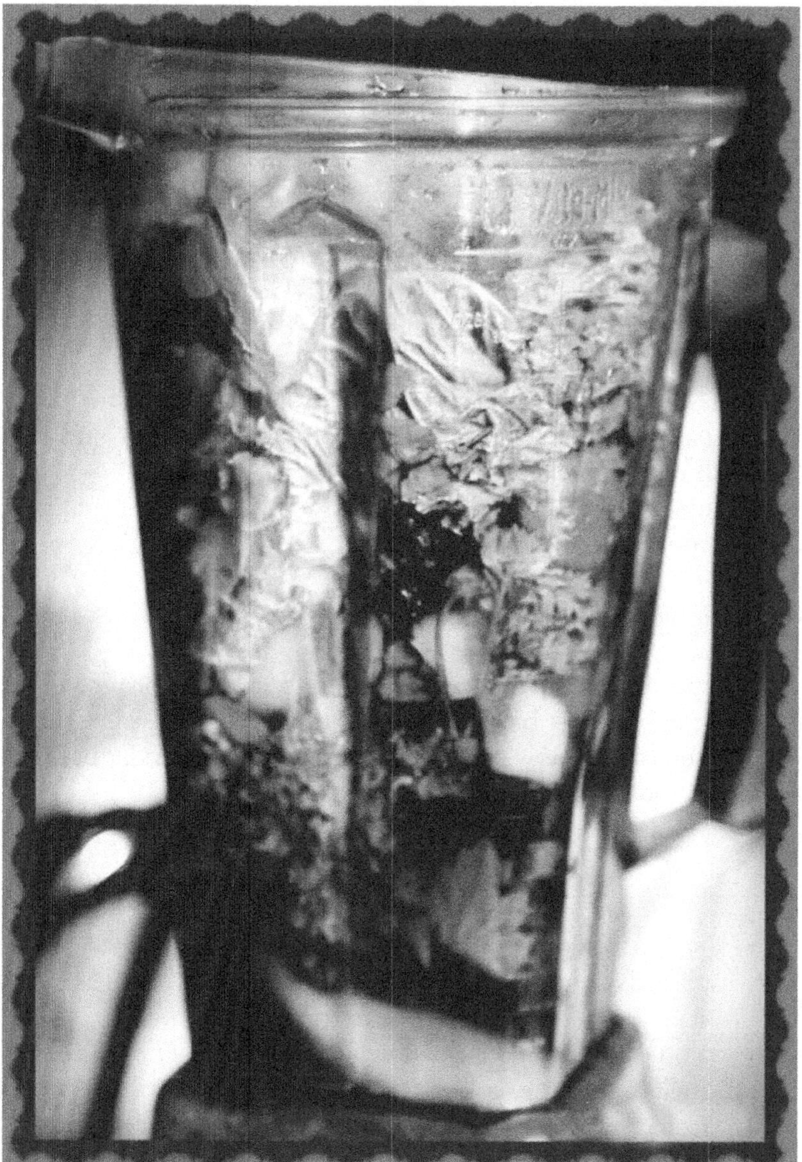

Step 1: Add Liquid

- Add 2-3 cups water or non-dairy milk into your blender container (depending on your container size, make it about 1/3rd of volume).

Optionally add:

- 1/4 whole lemon, including peel
- 1/4 cup raw, organic agave nectar or maple syrup
- 2-3 tablespoons ground flax seeds, raw nuts or other seeds * (see note below), superfoods (spirulina, maca), or nut/seed butter
- up to 1 cup of grains (quick oats, cooked quinoa, etc.), tofu or cooked sweet potato

Blend on high until smooth.

* High-speed blenders may be able to grind up seeds or nuts during the blend cycle, but most blenders will not thoroughly pulverize the seeds. If that's the case, simply grind them up in a coffee grinder before adding to your smoothie.

Step 2: Add Greens

- 1/2 to 1 lb raw, washed greens, such as spinach, kale, chard, collards, lettuce, etc. Non-starchy vegetables, such as celery stalks and cucumbers, are also excellent.
- You can blend greens whole; however, it's better to remove the stalks from kale, collards, and chard as they add a peppery taste to the smoothie. Tangy greens, such as dandelion greens, arugula, turnip, should be avoided or sparingly, as they are spicy and sometimes bitter (definitely not for beginners).
- Fresh herbs, such as parsley, cilantro, mint, or other, to taste.
- 1/2 of avocado for creaminess.

The container should be almost full before blending. Blend the greens until smooth.

Blending this way allows the dry ingredients to be mixed for longest, it means the greens will fit in your blender, and your fruit gets less blending, so it doesn't become too hot.

The blender should be about 2/3 full AFTER pureeing the greens. This is going to be some very green mixture!

Step 3: Add Fruit

Add fruit until the container is full. My favorite fruits for smoothies are bananas, mangoes, pears, peaches, strawberries, raspberries, and blueberries.

Note: If you are worried about the smoothie exploding when you switch the blender on again, you may pour part of the mixture into a glass, and then start adding the fruit.

- 1-2 very ripe bananas to add a creamy texture and sweetness
- 1-2 cups frozen or fresh mixed berries
- Any other fresh or frozen fruit to taste, such as pears, peaches, apples, mango, apricots, cantaloupes, pineapples, kiwi, or other.

Blend till mixture is very smooth. How long you blend will depend on your blender. I rarely blend for more than 10-20 seconds on high using my Vitamix, but you may need to blend for 20-30 seconds or even more. Pour into a glass and enjoy.

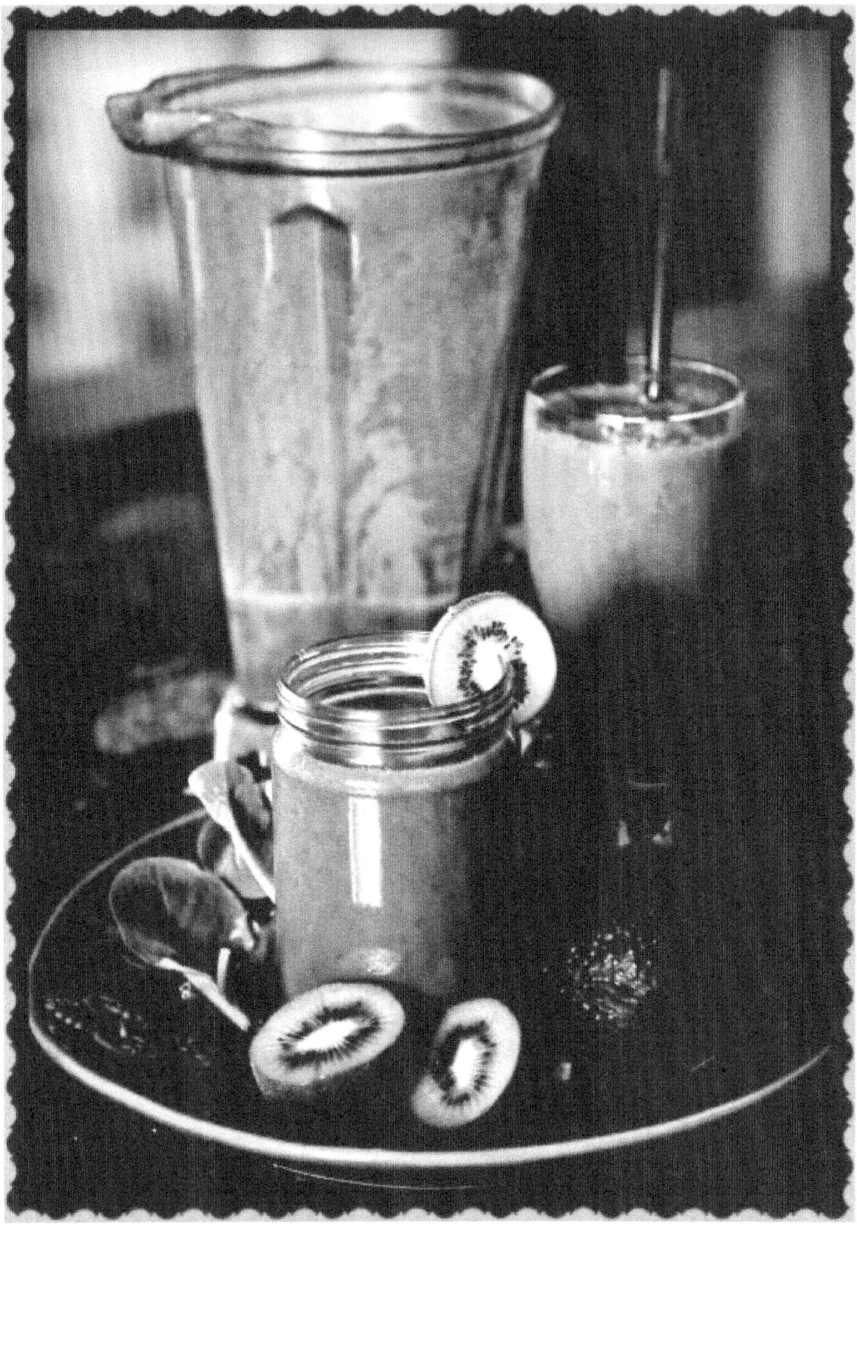

More tips

* Add more water if required to thin it out.

* Add ice if you prefer chilled, slushy-style smoothie. We drink our smoothies at room temperature most of the year, except hot summer months.

* If your smoothie gets too warm due to the prolonged blending, you can cool it down in the fridge or freeze some of your ingredients before blending. You can also replace half of the liquids with ice. Add the ice at the end. It is better to add frozen ingredients at the end to cool the smoothie down.

* Fruits that are rich in soluble fiber and pectin such as grains, citrus, apples, and berries, will make your smoothie creamy and will prevent the separation of liquid and fiber in the smoothie.

* If you don't like the frothy appearance of your smoothie, adding a cube or two of ice may help. The most likely cause of foam is apples, especially if they are not thoroughly blended. Frothiness in your smoothie does not reduce its nutritional value, so you can simply shake it or stir it before drinking to reduce bubbles and separation.

* If your smoothie is not sweet enough, add more fruits, or add some agave syrup or stevia. If you desire a less sweet tasting smoothie, next time, use more vegetables. Adjust water quantity to your liking.

* You can save your smoothie in the fridge for up to two days—just give it a good shake before drinking. You may also freeze a smoothie—just remember to take it out in advance to allow it the time to melt.

* Remind your kids (and everyone else) to drink your smoothie slowly, "chewing" the content to allow it to blend with your saliva for best digestion.

7 Tips for Successful Smoothie Routine

1. Prepare your smoothie first thing in the morning in the amount that your family usually consumes in one day, 1/2 quart or more per child, one or two quarts per adult.

Pour enough smoothie into a glass for everyone to drink in the morning, and keep the rest in the refrigerator or another cold place, but not the freezer. If you are going places and want to take your smoothie with you, put it in a bottle or coffee mug. That way, you minimize the chance of spilling it, and—if you use non-transparent containers—others will not notice the green color of your drink.

2. Drink your smoothie by itself, not as part of a meal.

To get the most nutritional benefits of your green smoothie, don't consume anything with it. You can eat anything you want about 30-40 minutes after your smoothie.

3. Sip your smoothies slowly, mixing it with saliva for better digestion.

4. Stick to the basic green smoothie recipes as much as possible, i.e., smoothies made with leafy greens and ripe fruits only, especially if you have digestive issues.

Even though I provide some recipes for smoothies that contain starchy vegetables, nuts, seeds, grains, etc., all these ingredients slow down the assimilation of nutrients in your digestive tract and may cause gas for some people.

5. Don't put too many ingredients into one smoothie, such as five different fruits and five different greens.

I admit I often break this rule putting lots of different ingredients into my blender, but many times simple is better.

6. Try various recipes and perfect the ones you like best.

If your learn to prepare delicious smoothies, chances are you will stick with your routine, as you will always be looking forward to the next one.

7. Choose locally grown, organic ingredients whenever possible, and choose fruits that are fully ripe.

Ripe, organic, locally grown are best. I write more on shopping organic in the Buying Organic section). However, don't skip your smoothie routine just because organic produce is not available.

Troubleshooting a Smoothie

It happens rarely, but it does happen. You made a smoothie that your child doesn't care for. I'm not talking about children or adults who are new to the idea of smoothies (if that's the case, refer to Tips To Get Your Kids Started With Green Smoothies section).

I'm talking here about *seasoned* smoothie (and especially *green* smoothie) drinkers, like my 9-year-old-son, who has been drinking about a quart of smoothie per day since he was four. He rarely complains and almost never refuses to drink the smoothie that I make for him; however, it does happen on occasion.

Fortunately, the advantage of smoothies over other types of recipes, such as baking, is that they can be easily fixed.

How to Fix A Green Smoothie That You or Your Child Don't Love

It may take a little experimentation to make the smoothie perfectly to your child's liking. Some children will be easy to please, while some will refuse to drink the smoothie until it's fine-tuned to perfection. Sort of like Goldilocks' "just right!"

Here are some objections that you may hear from time to time, and how to address them:

"My smoothie is too thick to drink with a straw!"

Enjoy it with a spoon! Or simply add more liquid to thin it out to desired consistency. The best liquid for smoothies is water, but any non-dairy milk, coconut water, or fresh juice can be used as well.

"My smoothie is too watery!"

Add more fruits and veggies! Bananas and avocados are great for making thick smoothies that are nice and creamy. A good way to makes sure your recipe is just to your liking is to start by adding only half of the liquid that the recipe calls for. Then, slowly add the remaining liquid until the desired thickness is achieved. Adding some nut or seed butter, oats or cooked quinoa is another way to add a delicious creaminess to a smoothie. (See section on Rich & Creamy Smoothies)

"My smoothie is not sweet enough!"

Add more sweet fruits, such as half a banana, a few grapes, or a piece of pear. A few dates or other dried fruit will also work, but you'll have to blend them well to avoid complaints about " *chunky*" smoothie. As a last resort, try adding 1-2 tablespoons maple syrup or another sweetener. (See my section on Sweeteners for smoothies)

"My smoothie is too sweet."

It's rare, but I hear this complaint from time to time. If it does, squeeze some lemon or lime juice into the smoothie. Add a tart apple or an orange and blend well. Or add more greens and/or celery.

"My smoothie is yucky."

This usually means that the smoothie is too *"green" tasting*. Some greens have a very distinct flavor, so if you added too much of them, the taste would be too strong. Dilute the smoothie by adding more fruits, mild greens, and some condiments, such as ginger, lemon, vanilla, or cinnamon.

"My smoothie has a yucky color."

The best way to mask the color is to add some frozen blueberries or cocoa powder to the mix. Another way is to serve it in a non-transparent container with a straw.

"My smoothie just doesn't taste good."

If there is no specific issue that can be pinpointed, perhaps you added too many ingredients that don't complement each other, or not enough ingredients that have a distinct taste. Whatever the reason, I find that adding spices, such as cinnamon, vanilla, a piece of fresh ginger, a slice of lemon (or some lemon juice), or a few fresh mint leaves will add some instant zing to any smoothie that is too bland.

Once you have the problem fixed, here is what will happen:

Worst comes to worst, you'll have the smoothie all to yourself. (Or give it to your spouse.)

Top Sweeteners for the Smoothies

1. The fresh fruit itself!

Raw, ripe sweet fruit is the best sweetener of all for your smoothies. Humans are naturally drawn to sweet foods. We are just so bombarded with overly sweet processed foods that make eating a juicy, crisp apple may seem like a chore. Help your child learn to drink fruit smoothies without the stimulating sugars added. You will be surprised at how quickly everyone's taste buds will become adjusted to the subtle, yet delicious, flavors of fruit.

2. Dates and other dried fruits

Use them dried or pre-soak them before adding to your smoothie. Keep in mind that some blenders may not blend dried fruit entirely, leaving some chunks in the smoothie.

3. Agave, Fruit Juice, Maple Syrup, or Molasses

Other good options are agave, fruit juice, maple syrup, or molasses.

4. Stevia (the Herb)

If calories are a concern, you may consider Stevia as your sweetener. Stevia is an extraordinarily sweet herb -- about 200-300 times sweeter than sugar, and it's almost calorie-free. It has a slight licorice-like flavor that most people enjoy. Stevia has a negligible effect on blood glucose, even enhancing glucose tolerance; therefore, it is attractive as a natural sweetener to diabetics and others on diets. It does not cause cavities, and you won't get a sudden burst of energy followed by fatigue and a need for another "fix." It also does not feed yeast or other microorganisms. It is available in several forms, including powder, crushed green leaves, and a crude greenish-brown syrup. You can find Stevia in the health food store or health section of your grocery (please, don't confuse it with Splenda, an artificial sweetener, definitely NOT recommended).

5. Yacon and Lucuma

These are two "superfood" sweeteners that come in powdered and in a syrup form. Both of them are roots originating from South America. They're sweet with a hint of caramel/molasses flavor. They are also low glycemic sweeteners. They are carbohydrates that bypass the metabolism, so we don't get spikes in blood sugar—another excellent option for people with diabetes and anybody else that's being conscientious about the amount of sugar that they're eating.

The Bottom Line

Try to enjoy your smoothies (and other food) without sweeteners. Fresh fruit and occasionally a little date sugar or dates is the best way to go. Use sweeteners sparingly.

Boosting Your Smoothies With Sprouts

Growing sprouts is an easy and fun way to get fresh greens during the winter months. It is also a fun way for the kids to learn some science.

Sprouts are some of the most incredibly nutritious, affordable, and easy to grow foods. They provide a steady year-round source of vitamins, minerals, trace minerals, enzymes, antioxidants, chlorophyll, and protein, as well as a high concentration of health and youth-supporting enzymes. As some of the most nutritious foods that exist, they make a great addition to any healthy eating plan.

You can have them fresh all year round, even when fresh vegetables are hard to find. It's much easier than planting a garden outside, and they're ready much quicker. It takes less than 2 minutes a day, and they are ready in 3 to 7 days, depending on the variety. I like to use an organic salad mix of red clover, alfalfa, kale, and radish that I get on Sproutman.com.

Use them in smoothies, blended soups, and salads, as well as regular salads, on sandwiches, stir-fried with vegetables, or enjoy these nutrient-packed delicacies as a snack all by themselves or added as a garnish to the main dish.

To make a smoothie, add about 1/4 to 1/2 cup of sprouts to any smoothie recipe. Don't put too many sprouts in your smoothie, to avoid an overwhelmingly grassy flavor. Used in moderation, however, and sprouts are an absolute delight.

Spring Sprout Smoothie
1/4 cup alfalfa sprouts
1 cup baby spinach
1 cup pineapple, fresh or frozen
1 banana
1 cup of water
1/4" – 1/2" fresh ginger, minced
1 teaspoon of agave nectar (optional)

Blend ingredients in a powerful blender until smooth and creamy. Thin with water or thicken with ice if desired. Enjoy!

How to Grow Sprouts with Your Kids

Growing sprouts in your kitchen is a fun thing to do with your kids. Sprouts are easy to grow and take a minimum of effort. You probably already have everything you need to start your kitchen garden.

To grow sprouts in jars on your kitchen sink, you will need:

- a wide-mouth jar, screen or netting, and a rubber band
- a special plastic tray
- sprouting seeds

Buying organically grown sprouting seeds is recommended (see the resources section at the end of the book). Seeds that are not specifically for sprouting and are not organic may be chemically treated with pesticides. Even though organic seeds may be a little more expensive, keep in mind that two ounces of seeds will yield 1-2 pounds of sprouts, so you'll get a lot of sprouts from just a handful of seeds.

How to grow your sprouts:

Note: Your indoor garden will grow best when the temperature is between 65°F and 75°F (18°C and 25°C).

1. Put 1 to 2 tablespoons of seeds in a wide-mouth jar.

2. Cover with netting or cheesecloth and secure with a rubber band.

3. Rinse a couple of times, then fill the jar 3/4 full with filtered water at room temperature, and soak 6-8 hours or overnight.

4. Drain water. Rinse 2 or 3 times in cool water.

5. Transfer the seeds to a sprouting tray and spread them evenly on the surface. (You can sprout the seeds in a jar or a bag, but I find special plastic trays much more convenient.)

6. Rinse 2 or 3 times twice a day in cool water.

7. Place the sprouting tray in bright light, but not direct sunlight, the last sprouting day to allow chlorophyll to form.

8. Sprouts will grow three to seven days. Seed sprouts, like alfalfa or red clover, are 1" (2.5 cm) to 2" (5 cm) long when ready. They should be watered/rinsed 3-4 times a day. Taste the sprouts as they are growing to see when you like them best.

9. You may refrigerate your sprouts to store.

my sprouting garden

Is Buying Organic Produce Important?

Organic produce for green smoothies and juicing is not always easy to find, plus it often costs considerably more than conventionally grown fruits and vegetables.

While consuming conventional fruits and vegetables is always better than not consuming any plant foods at all, when you really study what you are digesting when eating conventionally grown foods and the effects these chemicals have on our health and environment, it clearly shows the benefits of choosing organic.

Many studies demonstrate that most conventionally grown foods contain pesticides and other chemical residues. Many of these foods literally carry "a cocktail of synthetic poisons." A growing body of research is showing that repeated exposures to cocktails of small amounts of synthetic chemicals have a range of adverse health effects, especially for children. Many of these substances are endocrine disruptors, which can cause a host of health problems, including congenital disabilities, all kinds of cancers, diabetes, obesity, autism, and others.

The Dirty Dozen: Buy Organic If Possible

So here is the list of the so-called Dirty Dozen, the foods that are most contaminated, so it's best to only buy organic: **celery, peaches, strawberries, apples, blueberries, nectarines, sweet bell peppers, leafy greens: spinach, kale, and collard greens, cherries, potatoes, grapes (imported), and lettuce.**

The Clean 15: Produce Lowest in Pesticides

Not all non-organic fruits and vegetables have a high pesticide level. Some produce has a strong outer layer that provides a defense against pesticide contamination non-organic fruits, and vegetables dubbed the "Clean 15" that contained little to no pesticides: **avocados, sweet corn, pineapples, mango, sweet peas, asparagus, kiwi fruit, cabbage, eggplant, cantaloupe, watermelon, grapefruit, sweet potatoes, sweet onions, honeydew, and melon.**

However, even in the case of these foods, I encourage you to buy organic whenever possible. The damaging effect that toxic pesticides and herbicides, as well as synthetic fertilizers, have on the soil and the environment are massive, so please support sustainable, organic agriculture whenever you can.

To limit your exposure, it makes sense to peel fruits, if possible, and not to eat skins, unless you are able to purchase those vegetables in organic form. Remove and discard the outermost leaves of lettuce and cabbage, and other surfaces that can't be peeled, can be washed with soap and water or a commercial vegetable wash.

Still, as alarming as this may sound, we need to keep the problem of pesticides in perspective. If you have a choice between a piece of meat or a cup of non-organic strawberries, the strawberries are better and less toxic food, as the meat concentrates far more toxin from pesticides than any plant produce.

Another point to remember is that organically produced fruits and vegetables contain **much higher amounts of nutrients**, and therefore are more nutrition-rich and health-promoting, than their conventional counterparts.

It may not always be possible, but if you have a local farmer's market in your neighborhood, do most of your shopping there. Locally produced, seasonal foods cut energy use and therefore leave a smaller impact on the environment. It's also usually fresher and more nutritious. Or just grow your own greens and veggies—it doesn't get more local than that.

A Note About Blenders

To make green smoothies, all you need is the ingredients and a blender. You can make smoothies with any blender, so don't feel like you have to spend a lot of money on a new machine to begin blending your smoothies.

However, if you are shopping for a new blender, I recommend buying the most powerful blender you can find and afford, 1,000 watts or more. A high-speed blender, such as Vitamix or Blendtec, is best because it will break the cell walls of even the toughest greens, making absorbing nutrients easier on the body. They do a terrific job, and they last forever. Yes, they are quite costly but think about it as an investment in your family's health. Just consider how much money you will save on medical bills and medications!

Everyone who ever used a Blendtec or Vitamix admits that these two blenders are in the class of their own. They blend stuff like you've never seen before. AND....they aren't just a blender. They are all-in-one appliances that make smoothies, juice, ice cream, margaritas, soups, sauces, breads, dressings, salsas, and more. Baby food can be pureed better than with the food processor. With these blenders, you can blend, chop, grind, cook, crush, mince, dice, mill, purée, and more, replacing multiple appliances with one easy-to-use tool. Both machines are used in restaurants, coffee shops, juice bars, gyms, and health clubs. The reason for this popularity is simple: they are known for producing great, consistent results in taste and texture of blended foods.

If you don't have a powerful blender, you can still make green smoothies and benefit from them, but you will have to chop your ingredients into smaller pieces, blend for longer periods of time, and put up with some chunks in your smoothie. Taste is going to be very different and the texture is going to be very different than with one of these more high-powered tools, but it's better than nothing.

How to Save Money When Buying a Blender

If you are on a tight budget but want to buy a Vitamix or Blendtec, it's worth to shop around. You can buy a refurbished Vitamix at a lower price. Or, even better, you can find these power blenders on places like eBay or Craigslist. People sell them for cheap because they bought them, or somebody else bought it for them, and they didn't use them.

Noise Reduction Secret

These blenders are powerful, no question about it, but some people complain that they are loud—so here is a noise reduction trick that works for any loud counter-top appliance. What to do? Just put a few mouse-pads under the blender and enjoy!

Smoothie Ingredients: Cheat Sheet

Greens & Raw Veggies

- Leafy Greens: Arugula, beet greens (tops), bok choy, broccoli leaves, carrot tops, celery, chard, collard greens, dandelion, endive, escarole, kale, Romaine, green and red leaf lettuce, Boston lettuce, radicchio, radish tops, spinach.
- Sprouts: Alfalfa, broccoli, clover, fenugreek, radish, sunflower.
- Raw Vegetables: Asparagus, broccoli, carrots, celery stalks, cucumber (with the skin on or off), okra, squash, zucchini, etc.
- Herbs: Aloe vera, basil, cilantro, chives, dill, fennel, mint, parsley, spearmint, and others.
- Start with 20% and work up to 50% ratio of greens and veggies in green smoothies.

Fruits (Fresh, frozen or dried)

- Acai berries, apples, apricots, bananas, blackberries, blueberries, cherries, cranberries, figs, grapefruit, grapes, kiwifruit, lemons, limes, mangos, melon, oranges, papaya, peaches, pears, pineapple, plums, pomegranate, raspberries, strawberries, watermelon, and other.
- Avocado (yes, it's a fruit, low in sugar, high in healthy fats).
- Start with up to 80% of fruits in green smoothies. Or substitute some of the fruit with whole grains and/or sweetener.

Raw Nuts and Seeds; or Nut/Seed Butters

- Almonds, Brazil nuts, cashews, hazelnuts, macadamia, pine nuts, pecans, walnuts. Chia, flax, pumpkin, sesame, sunflower, tahini, etc. If your child is allergic to nuts, raw seeds, and seed butters are a great alternative. Optionally, to boost your healthy fat intake. 1-3 tablespoons per quart.

Adding Bulk: Whole Grains, Cooked Vegetables, & Legumes

- Whole grains (cooked or sprouted): Oats (quick-oats don't need to be cooked); cooked brown rice, quinoa, millet, etc. Cooked or raw starchy vegetables: Cooked sweet potato, pumpkin, or squash. Tofu or sprouted legumes. You can even add cooked legumes to smoothies, such as chickpeas or white beans. Optionally, to add more bulk and make smoothies more filling & nutritious.

Liquids

- Water, freshly made juice, coconut water, or any non-dairy milk: almond milk, hemp milk, oat milk, organic soy milk, etc. Rejuvelac (a probiotic drink made from grains). Add 1-3 cups to reach desired consistency.

Sweeteners

- Fresh fruit, dried fruit, and occasionally a little date sugar is the best way to go. If you want an even sweeter smoothie, add Stevia (the herb), agave, fruit juice, maple syrup, or molasses.
- Use sparingly. Try to enjoy your smoothies without them.

Turbo-Charge Taste & Nutrition with Spices & Superfoods

- Cinnamon, carob powder, cocoa, vanilla. Fresh ginger and lemon peel are excellent to add zing to a smoothie.
- Maca, green powders, spirulina, hemp protein powder, vegan protein powders, etc.) Optionally.

Ice

- Add ice for a chilled smoothie (if not using frozen fruits).
- Note: Most of the time, I like to serve my smoothies at room temperature, and when adding lots of frozen ingredients, I add some warm or hot water to bring the smoothie to body temperature.

7 Ways to Save Money on Ingredients

Some of the tips may be well known to you, but I hope that you'll learn something new from this section!

1. Buying in bulk

Membership at a price-club, such as BJ's or Costco can help bring the cost down. I usually buy loads of bananas and organic spinach, as well as big bags of frozen mixed berries (organic) and wild blueberries.

2. Buying at co-ops and local markets

Look for the co-op groups in your area. They usually have great deals on organic produce. Moreover, you'll get better quality, locally grown produce. A melon that has been grown locally (local farms) will always taste better than a melon that had to be shipped more than 1,000 miles.

3. Growing your own fruits, veggies, and greens

Growing your fruits, vegetables and greens is a great way to make green smoothies easy on the pocket. It's a great outdoor activity for the whole family. It also gives you full control over the quality of the produce, as you use organic gardening methods very easily. Learning to garden will make your produce virtually free, and even if you don't have a garden, it's easy to grow greens in small spaces—on a patio or even a balcony.

4. Sprouting

With just a few jars or sprouts bags, some water, and just a little effort, you can grow your own sprouts, transforming highly nutritious seeds into delicious living vegetables packed with vitamins, minerals, protein, phytonutrients, fiber, and enzymes for the body—right in your kitchen. See the section on Sprouting.

5. Buying produce that's in season

By creating a grocery list for each season, you will get the most produce for your money. Fruits and vegetables that are in season will always be cheaper than produce that is not in season. Buying produce in season, even organic, will always cost less, thus keeping more money in your pockets. Plus, you'll get better quality, locally grown produce.

6. Picking wild greens and fruits

Depending on where you live, this may be a fun activity to do with your kids. At first, it may seem challenging to you if you never picked up wild edible plants, but picking and eating wild edibles can be fun, healthful, economical, and safe when done right. Wild edible plants often contain more vitamins and minerals than commercially produced plants.

While there are many benefits associated with eating wild foods, there are also some risks. You need to use caution when harvesting wild foods. First of all, you will need to learn how to identify edible plants. If you are ever unsure about whether a particular plant is edible or not, please, don't pick it. Also, don't pick from highly polluted and/or herbicide sprayed areas.

7. Substituting ingredients in recipes for lower-cost ingredients

Learn to substitute expensive ingredients with ingredients that are inexpensive where you live. For example, using flax seeds instead of chia seeds will work in most recipes, and flax seeds are much cheaper where I live. Celery tops are quite inexpensive and will work great in most recipes. Oats are very economical to use, and you can add more of them to your smoothie, replacing avocados, bananas, etc.

Q&A

How many calories are in your smoothies? Where's the nutrition information?

At this time, I do not post calorie counts or nutrition info for my smoothie recipes. This book is aimed at families, and I don't believe in counting calories for kids *(or even for adults)*. I think the best thing you can do as a parent is to try to provide your child with food choices that are made up of fresh, real, unprocessed foods, and if you do, then everything else will work itself out.

What's the recommended portion size?

Aim for at least half quart of smoothie per child, and one quart of smoothie per adult per day. This can be divided into two or three servings during the day. You can make the whole pitcher in the morning and store it in the fridge for later.

When making smoothies, keep in mind that measuring produce, especially greens can be tricky, and recipes will yield different results depending on how tightly packed your greens are, whether they are chopped, fresh or frozen, etc.

Adjust the amount of greens depending on your audience, starting with a little, and boosting it with more as their taste-buds adjust. Add more or less liquid depending on your preference for thicker or thinner smoothies.

How to store the smoothie?

You can save time by making smoothies in advance and storing them in the fridge. The smoothie will usually stay "good" for up to 3 days. You may give it a little shake or stir if separation occurs.

Why is there no dairy in the recipes?

Every smoothie recipe in this book is one hundred percent plant-based, vegan. Vegan smoothies are free of the animal products you often find in smoothie recipes, such as milk, dairy yogurt, and honey. Dairy from animals can contain saturated fat, hormones, chemicals, and more. Plus, many people experience problems with digesting dairy or are lactose intolerant. Milk is also linked to type 1 (juvenile-onset) diabetes and other serious conditions.

As far as calcium, according to Dr. Joel Fuhrman, a renowned physician specializing in nutrition and the author of the highly recommended book "Disease-Proof Your Child," when you eat a healthy diet rich in natural foods, fruits, vegetables, beans, nuts, and seeds, it is impossible not to obtain sufficient calcium. You may find comfort in knowing that leafy greens are the nutrient densest foods on this planet, and they contain plenty of calcium. Even the American Dietetic Association (ADA) agrees that properly planned (as they all should be) vegan diet is appropriate for all ages.

What's more, by choosing to avoid animal products in your smoothies, you will be making a compassionate choice for animals. This way of eating is better for all living beings, both human and non-human, and is better for the planet. It's a way of eating that adds compassion, kindness, and care for all living beings to the blend.

Just give these recipes a try, and you may find that you don't miss dairy at all.

References

(1) http://www.pbhfoundation.org/pdfs/about/res/pbh_res/stateplate.pdf

(2) https://www.drfuhrman.com/library/article5.aspx

(3) http://www.cdc.gov/healthyyouth/nutrition/facts.htm

(4) http://www.diseaseproof.com/archives/healthy-food-calcium-supplements-no-help-for-kids-bones.html

More Reading

Green Reset! 6-Week Green Smoothie and Juicing Challenge (with recipes, shopping lists, tips, detox advice, and more) (Green Reset Formula Book 1)

Easy Raw Soups: 30+ Super-Easy, Super-Healthy Raw Food Recipes Bursting With Flavor and Compassion! (Green Reset Formula Book Book 3)

Easy Soups! Creamy, Thick & Satisfying Soups That Fill You Up Without Compromising Your Waistline, Blood Sugar, Cholesterol or Ethics (Green Reset Formula Book 4)

Your Free Gift Is Waiting!

Get the "Green Reset Challenge"
with 7-Day Green Smoothie Challenge
with Green Reset Formula (with recipes, shopping lists, tips, detox advice, and more)

Go to JoannaSlodownik.com/gift/

Made in the USA
Las Vegas, NV
13 January 2024